HAVE YOU GOT *GOOD* RELIGION?

THE REAL FRUIT OF ISLAM

HAVE YOU GOT *GOOD* RELIGION?

THE REAL FRUIT OF ISLAM

by

Haman Cross, Jr., and Donna E. Scott

with Eugene Seals, editor

A Quality Book™

Published by Moody Press, Chicago, and
The Spoken Word, Detroit, Michigan 48223

By arrangement with Quality Publishing Systems, Inc.
Box 339635, Farmington Hills, Michigan 48333

1 3 5 7 9 10 8 6 4 2

Printed in the United States of America

Contents

Authors' Intent

It is not our intent to offend our precious Black Muslim brothers and sisters but to:

- Respectfully compare the two most vocal religious alternatives presented to the Black community
- Share the truth as we see it
- Have readers act upon the truth as they hear it
- Stimulate readers to research these truths legitimately and experientially

A DIVINE COMEDY?

What is the first thing that comes to mind when you think of Purgatory, Sheol, Gehenna, Hades, Tartaros, or Hell? The ancient Greeks mythologized this lower world to be the realm of spirits. The Hebrews say Hell originated just south of Jerusalem, where the filth and the dead were cast out and burned.

Italian poet Dante fancied this nether world to be a temporary Inferno several steps beneath paradiso. Early Egyptians referred to it as *Tuat*, situated under the earth. Christians believe that Hell is ruled by the Devil, while the Nation of Islam maintains that it's whatever you make it.

Regardless of the definition you and I conjure up, one fact is certain: Hell is very real. It is a place of suffering, punishment, misery, discord, anguish, and agony. No one in his or her right mind wants to go there.

The Greeks put a coin in the mouth of their loved ones in hopes that Charon, the boatman, would ferry their souls across the River Styx. Ancient Egyptians looked to Herfhaf to transport them to the desired land of Osirus. Dante relied on the Latin poet Virgil's guidance through the dark forest of terror into the empyrean realm of Heaven, where his beloved Beatrice awaited.

But who can those experiencing a "living hell" depend on? Who will mentor the bright management trainee, whose career is going nowhere simply because of his dark complexion? Who will lead the battered wife away from the cruel blows of her drunken husband? Who will offer poor, downtrodden, so-called social misfits a career change that offers more than perfunctory chores and minimum wages? What is their route to a happy ending?

Picture twenty-eight million people dying to know the path from this place of no return. For years their lives have had minimal praise, joy, and satisfaction. If they don't find an answer soon, more and more will look to deceivers, clairvoyants, and necromancers to grant them asylum.

C. S. Lewis, former Cambridge professor of medieval and Renaissance literature, insisted that people too easily give up. They erroneously believe that the God of the Bible is not interested in meeting their desires, that somehow He has abandoned them to the outer world of unmet needs, unfulfilled dreams, and unrequited love (Lewis, 4).

Blacks are on the outside; but we want in, desperately. However, we cannot seem to escape the pull of the nether world, the hell of unemployment, the pit of being undereducated, or the abyss of gang violence. Despite our inward groanings, satisfaction eludes us. Where is our Herfhaf who knows the way past daddy's incest? Where is our aged boatman Charon who will ferry our family out of financial ruin? Where is our guardian angel Beatrice when justice has closed its eyes to brutality?

After years of frustration and anguish, Black Americans have come to a fork in the road. On it are affixed two signs representing two belief systems. One points to the Nation of Islam. The other points to Christianity. Each promises that it is the true pathway toward an abundant life for our people. This creates a vexing dilemma for us.

The directions are mutually exclusive. Which road should we follow? Which direction will lead us away from the insidious cancer of racism, the hell of sexual abuse, and the suffocating pressure of ghetto life? To steer clear of the fire and brimstone of this life and the next, the superior belief system must provide the following escape components:

A map that is precise (the Quran or the Bible)

A model that is pure (Farrakhan or Jesus)

A method that is practical (works or grace)

A motivation that is powerful (hate or love)

This book examines which institution, the Nation of Islam or Christianity, is divinely inspired and indispensable to the salvation and deliverance of Black America from the pit of financial, spiritual, sociological, and emotional misery. We show the attributes the Nation and its Minister Farrakhan hold in common with other modern messianic movements. Using widely accepted disciplines of law, history, and journalism, we expose the highly exaggerated claims of Minister Farrakhan.

In the process, we answer the most pressing questions facing Black America. Which book, the Quran or the Bible, is the Word of God ? Which leader, Farrakhan or Christ, is the deliverer sent from the God of the Bible? Which method, works or grace, can save us from both a hellish existence and a hellish eternity? Which motivation, love or hate, is the most powerful agent for positive change?

But, in the final analysis, it is you, the reader, who must sit as the jury to render the verdict as to whether you have got *good* religion or a bad counterfeit.

1

A Map That Is Precise

Through me the way that runs among the lost. . . . Abandon
every hope, who enter here.
                                    Canto 3, *Inferno*

Nothing can be more frustrating than being lost, particularly when you have a so-called map in your possession. For instance, suppose your next-door neighbor, who just happens to be a pastor, has been encouraging you to visit his congregation. Since you are "fishing" for religion, you finally accept his invitation and jot down the directions so you can attend church the following Sunday. En route you notice little inconsistencies between the freeway signs and the directions from the so-called man of God. What was supposed to take thirty minutes turns into a two-hour wilderness adventure.

Silently you criticize yourself for not having stopped at the gas station your conscience tried to guide you toward two exits earlier. But since it was a holy man who told you the way, you doggedly follow the instructions anyway – that is until you come to a fork in the road that the reverend neglected to mention! So far, this road to a taste of heaven has given you nothing but hell. Exasperated, you scream out, "Which way?"

Similarly, twenty-eight million Black Americans are at a fork in the road where they are being offered two maps – one from the Nation of Islam and a completely different one from the Christian church. Both promise to get us to our desired destination. But our gut tells us that something is wrong.

Lost and Found. *If* there is a heaven, where can it be found? Certainly not in South Central L.A. or in the many red-lined urban areas, which are as American as apple pie. How can Black Americans find the place of rest and acceptance where there is no more pain, where our tears will be wiped away, and where we can find sanctuary from abusers of civil liberties?

In *The Evergreen Wood*, based on John Bunyan's fabled *Pilgrim's Progress*, Christopher Mouse braves dark forests, steep hills, black valleys, and other pitfalls to reach a place of peace and safety (Parry, 6-10). Black Americans' journey has been no different. We have endured years of slavery, racism, and other abuses in search of dignity, identity, and freedom from oppression.

Our very roots in this country have included a unique dehumanization process that,

parallels the concentration camp experience of World War II. First, there was the shock of being captured and unceremoniously uprooted from familiar, friendly soil. Thirst, brutality, and near starvation punctuated the experience of each exhausted man and woman who was forced to participate in the awesome one-way trip from the interior to the coast. Second, there was the humiliation of being sold to foreign traders. Then came the stupefying Middle Passage from Africa to the Americas. This nightmare at sea involved severe overcrowding, frequent rape, fatal disease, and cruel beatings, all of which served to establish the master's absolute domination. This abuse had such an effect upon the unfortunate Africans that their personalities were altered to suit the image and likeness of a system that assumed their inferiority. (Salley and Behm, 18)

Abuse is tantamount to a living hell. Whether sexual, verbal, physical, emotional, or psychological, abuse can engender feelings of ambivalence, contempt, and powerlessness. There is no argument concerning the political, social, economic, theological, and emotional abuses Black Americans have suffered. Indeed, a plethora of books documents our loss of dignity, humanity, and place in a society that has destroyed our self-esteem from the days of chattel slavery even to the present.

Dan Allender, a leading lecturer on abuse, notes that after enduring endless violations to one's personhood "the feeling of despair that it will never stop increases. There is no hope. There is the impression that there is nothing you can do" (Allender, 100-139).

That was the feeling many Black Americans internalized when Rodney King's attackers were set free after the Simi Valley trial. That was the feeling of countless Black men when Malice Green lay dead in Detroit's streets. That was the fuel source that grew into the mother of all civil disturbances in L.A. with sympathy outbursts in places as far removed as Toronto, Ontario.

In light of the abuses to which Black Americans have been subjected, the question we must ask today is, How do we make it stop? How do we escape this present hell? Too many wounded Black hearts look for asylum in drugs, violence, sexual promiscuity, and, yes, religion.

Some choose the Nation of Islam. Others choose Christianity. But which is the most viable option? Or does it matter which you choose? After centuries of dehumanization and hardship, we cannot afford further victimization. Yet the probability that we will be psychologically, socially, emotionally, and physically assaulted in the future will increase without proper intervention (Russell, 159).

In the face of this alarming statistic, both the Nation of Islam and Christianity promise healing from the internal and external repercussions of wounds inflicted upon Black America. But which religion is most valid? Which can salve the sting of racism, the abuse of ghettoization? We cannot afford to be wrong, for there is nothing in hell that Blacks want. We are all too familiar with it in this life and want no part of it in the next.

Thus, before approving of either Christianity or the Nation of Islam, Black Americans must determine what each system actually teaches. This can be done best by evaluating the original sources, or holy books, to discern whether, indeed, they've got good religion.

Quran or Bible. Both the Quran and the Bible, the maps as it were for these competing belief systems, have graphic depictions of hell and describe ways to escape that ultimate inferno. The Quran describes hell as a place of utter darkness, the wretched home for evildoers. It goes on to say that hell is the domain where oppressors will be burned in boiling water, gored, and subjected to other kindred things (Sura 38:55-58).

The Bible, too, tells us that hell is a very real place, a place of torment, outer darkness, destruction, fire, and brimstone (Revelation 20:14; Proverbs 5:5). Yet, the most poignant description of hell is that it represents eternal separation from our holy and gracious God and His Son Jesus Christ in whose presence is indescribable bliss.

It is imperative that the map be precise, whether it be the map the Quran provides or the map the Judeo-Christian Scriptures provide. If Black Americans have an incorrect map, if they do not know where they are going, they stand to face not only a hellish existence on a daily basis but also a hellish eternity as well.

Grave Differences. According to the Islamic view of history, an angel from Allah inspired Mohammed to write the Quran (Morey, 76). Supposedly, this holy book is the latest revelation, the final authority. Yet both Muslim and Western scholars note grave differences between what the Quran has to say and what the Bible has to say.

For instance, both the Bible and the Quran attest to the fact that Jesus Christ lived, that He was a prophet and a man from the God of the Bible. But the Quran goes on to deny Jesus' resurrection (Morey, 135).

Because of space limitations, we can only give a brief survey of the comparisons between the Bible and the Quran. For a more exhaustive look at the subject, Muslim Ali Dashti's *23 Years* and Robert Morey's *Islamic Invasion* are excellent study tools.

Principles of Historiography. In his comprehensive apologetic on the Christian faith, Josh McDowell notes, "The historical reliability of scripture, be it the Quran or the Bible, should be tested by the same criteria by which all documents are tested" (McDowell, 39). C. Sanders explains three basic tests of historiography: the bibliographical test, the internal evidence test, and the external evidence test (81, 143ff).

Bibliographical Test. Since we do not have the original documents with us, this test asks how reliable the copies are in regard to the number of manuscripts. There are more than 24,000 manuscript copies or portions of the New Testament in existence today. The ancient document that has the next largest number of existing manuscripts is Homer's *Iliad,* with 634 surviving manuscripts. That doesn't even come close. In other words, 24,000 manuscripts corroborate Jesus' resurrection from the dead. And yet the Quran insists otherwise. This presents a dilemma in that Sura 2:136 claims that the Quran is a continuation of the Bible.

According to Morey, the results of the bibliographical test mean that whenever the Bible and the Quran have a conflict, the Quran is to give way (Morey, 134). In fact, Muslim and Western scholars agree that there are *no* reliable manuscripts of the Quran. What has been found was collected from stones, bark, palm leaves, animal ribs, wooden boards, and pieces of leather, according to such internationally regarded Muslim scholars as Mandidi (Morey, 110). Worse yet, Ali Dashti, himself a renowned Muslim scholar, notes that animals at times ate the palm leaves or mats on which the Suras of the Quran had been recorded. Perhaps this is what became of their documentation of Jesus' resurrection!

Needless to say, if you are trying to escape a hellish existence, you need a map that is complete and reliable, preferably one that can get you from point A to point B efficiently and effectively.

Sir Frederick G. Kenyon, a historical curator, notes that "the authenticity and general integrity of the books of the New Testament are finally established in terms of the validity of the New Testament as we have it today" (McDowell, 41). The Quran, on the other hand, is referred to as disjointed and irregular in character by the standard reference, *The Concise Encyclopedia of Islam* (Morey, 109). Furthermore, McClintock and Strong add:

(T)he Quran is exceeding incoherent and sententious, the book evidently being without any logical order or thought as a whole or in its parts. This agrees with the desultory and incidental manner in which it is said to have been delivered. (Morey, 108)

While the Bible leaves the reader with a sense of wholeness from the beginning of Genesis to the end in Revelation, the Quran renders one confused and lost from one Sura to the next.

Internal Evidence Test. The second principle of historiography requires literary critics to follow Aristotle's dictum: "Give the benefit of doubt to the document and not to the critics." This entails carefully listening to the claims of the document under analysis and not assuming fraud unless the author disqualifies himself by contradiction or known factual inaccuracy (McDowell, 61).

It also demands that one further scrutinize primary sources (eyewitnesses) for correct interpretations of passages and words. Unfortunately, because of his unexpected death, Mohammed, fabled author of the Quran, was unable to gather many of his scattered records, revelations, and Suras. Moreover, many of his followers who had committed his Suras to memory died in battle before recording what they had heard.

As a result of the demise of these primary sources and the irreverent ingestion of biodegradable sermons, mass confusion confronted many interpreters of quranic material. As might be expected, one person's story often contradicted another person's recollections (Morey, 111).

On the other hand, the New Testament has numerous eyewitness information accounts of the life, death, and resurrection of Jesus Christ. For instance, Luke writes, "Inasmuch as many have undertaken to compile an account of the things accomplished among us, just as those who from the beginning were eyewitnesses and servants of the word have handed them down to us, it seemed fitting for me as well, having investigated everything carefully from the beginning, to write it out for you in consecutive order" (Luke 1:1-3 NASB).

Peter adds, "For we did not follow cleverly devised tales when we made known to you the power and coming of our Lord Jesus Christ, but we were eyewitnesses of His majesty" (2 Peter 1:16 NASB). John states that, "What we have seen and heard we proclaim to you also, that you also may have fellowship with us; and indeed our fellowship is with the Father, and with His Son Jesus Christ" (1 John 1:3 NASB).

F. F. Bruce, former Professor of Biblical Criticism and Exegesis at the University of Manchester, notes concerning the primary source value of the New Testament :

> *The earliest preachers of the gospel knew the value of . . . first hand testimony and appealed to it time and again, friendly and non-friendly. Yet, the disciples could not afford to risk inaccuracies which would be exposed by those who would be glad to do so. The presence of hostile witnesses served as a further corrective as to not depart from the facts.* (McDowell, 62)

According to John Warwick Montgomery, law school dean, "The New Testament Scriptures could stand up under any court of law in the world today, even when applying the ancient document rule" (McDowell, 40).

External Evidence Test. The final principle of historiography involves finding out what sources apart from the document under analysis attest to the document's accuracy, reliability, and authenticity. The problem also concerns devout Muslims. Ali Dashti writes:

The Qor'an contains sentences which are incomplete and not fully intelligible without the aid of commentaries; foreign words, unfamiliar Arab words, illogical and ungrammatically applied pronouns . . . and over one hundred aberrations from the normal structure of Arabic writing. These and other such aberrations in the language have given scope to critics who deny the Qor'an's eloquence. (Dashti, 48)

Thomas Carlyle observes, "It also is as toilsome a reading as I ever undertook, a wearisome, confused jumble, crude and incondite. Nothing but a sense of duty could carry one through the Quran" (Morey, 108). Moreover, old manuscripts of the Quran are supposedly based on Shiite Muslim claims that Uthman left out 25 percent of the original verses in the Quran for political reasons and, in fact, destroyed the older copies to alleviate confusion (Morey, 125).

On the other hand, there is tremendous supporting evidence for the Bible. Irenaeus, former Bishop of Lyons and student of Polycarp, writes, "So firm is the ground upon which these gospels rest, that the very heretics themselves bear witness to them" (McDowell, 63). This is important because, again, if twenty-eight million Black Americans are relying on either the Quran or the Bible, these maps must be accurate.

Other Sources. The Nation of Islam uses other literary sources beside the Quran and the Bible. However, the sources used contradict one another on essential matters, creating more confusion for our people.

For example, Elijah Muhammad in *Message to the Black Man* insists that the Bible cannot be proved to be the word of Allah and that it is not holy. This was a reaction to a "White Christianity" that paved the way for racism. In fact, it is precisely the existence of centuries of racist attitudes and hostility against Blacks that made thinkers such as Muhammad seek solace in what Albert Cleage calls a "dehonkified" ideology that would put an end to the oppression of our people.

Their new holy book, or map, was purportedly more sensitive to Black children plagued by roaches, rats, and undernourishment, to Black youth living in dilapidated ghettos, and to Black men trying to survive in economic recessions. But, what would it profit a child or a man – or a nation, for that matter – to gain the whole world and lose his own soul? Or what would a Black American give in exchange for his own soul?

According to Columbus Salley, former director of the U.S. Department of Education, Black theologians have gone a long way toward defining a religion independent of oppressive White thinking. As important as this is, however, issues more substantive than the color of Christ's skin must be addressed.

Model for Change. Having a precise map is important, but having a knowledgeable guide, or a pure model, is even better. Among other things, the pure model must be devoid of racist attitudes, distorted ideologies, and selfish thinking. Such a model must possess the ability to identify with the current economic, political, theological, and sociological realities facing Black Americans. And if he is to lead Black Americans beside still waters, this model's true colors must be exposed. Specifically, do his roots stem from the tree of Jesse or from the tree of bitterness? We will dig for these answers next.

2

A Model That Is Pure

Oh my God, they're killing themselves!
Bob Ricks

On April 19, 1993, the world was shocked by the actions of self-styled messiah David Koresh who led eighty-six followers in what officials called a mass suicide by fire. The inferno ended a fifty-one-day standoff between authorities and the Branch Davidian religious sect. For many the horror was, in the words of Bruce Gent who lost four loved ones, "bloody unreal."

The Gents' daughter, Nicole, her two children, and her twin brother, Peter, were among those who perished. Walter Martin, an African American Harvard Law School graduate, and four of his seven children were also killed in the cult fire. In fact, only nine of the eighty-six cult members are believed to have survived. As authorities rummaged through the charred remains of the Waco, Texas, compound, the question everyone wanted to unearth was, Why?

Why would someone lead people who believed, loved, and trusted him to such a painful demise? Why would precious few cult members, such as Sheila Martin, be courageous enough to make the decision to leave her husband and four children behind when they chose to melt away in that fiery furnace? Why would forty Black Americans, already wounded by racism and oppression, expose themselves to further scarring by even joining the Branch Davidian cult? In fact, who in their right mind would follow this "wacko from Waco"?

Former Branch Davidians offered clues when they divulged that inside the Ranch Apocalypse compound the cult leader led his flock with a Bible in one hand and a gun in the other. Through his power of persuasion, Koresh convinced his followers that he was the Messiah, the Christ. He went so far as to convince men that only he had a right to sleep with their wives. His power of persuasion was so effective that nineteen women bore his offspring (Hall, 2A).

How can so many be manipulated? According to noted Black psychiatrist Dr. Alvin Poussaint, usually such persons are very religious, very lonely, dependent, and looking for a family, a group to which they can feel they belong and be somebody (Waldron, 12). This same fatal attraction can be seen among urban gang members who are hungry for attention, social acceptance, and interpersonal relationships. Sadly, this kind of dysfunctional extended family usually leads to violence and loss of life of which the Branch Davidian "boyz in the 'hood" represent an extreme case.

Poussaint also explains that cult followers show an absence of independent thought. They display blind faith, and it is difficult to reach them, especially when they are isolated and cut off from the world. Like gang members, they believe it's "us against them." Rev. Eric

Hooker, pastor of the Waco Second Baptist Church, agrees, observing that Blacks who get caught up in a cult are often misguided.

Given the history of discrimination and abuse against Black Americans, this should come as no surprise. "When a person or people have been abused and victimized," according to Allender, "they lose their freedom to choose. Since the abuse was neither wanted nor invited, its occurrence is not a choice. Whether it happened one time or hundreds of times, the fact does not change, choice is denied, powerlessness is experienced and dignity is assaulted" (Allender, 98). And because people lose their ability to choose, they can be easily misled by charmers promising eternal salvation from their present hellish situation. "Searching for something to hold onto, they become," in Hooker's words, "easy prey for false prophets."

For example, many prison inmates join various cults to prevent the incidence of assault. For some there are only two choices, either become abused or become religious. Therefore, their choices are often based on self-protection, not on an evaluation of the merits of each choice.

Whether it is Waco, prison, or a gang in South Central L.A., countless Black men are set up into following leaders who promise protection against the possibilities of further abuse, be it rape, murder, or racism. And because their sense of perspective is warped, these vulnerable, frightened people succumb to more unscrupulous hype.

Indeed, cult experts say that many who perished in the Waco fire believed that they were being saved from the satanic world on earth. They had built their lives around the leader and even when his practices didn't match his preaching, they were still unwilling to back out and run away from Koresh's influence. Dayton Hudson department store heir Betsy Dovydenas escaped Koresh's thought-reform environment, only after her parents hired a deprogrammer to get her out.

Many Black Americans, however, lack the family financial resources to escape a manipulator who exploits our emotional, physical, and social weaknesses, thereby penetrating our very soul. To escape the hellish existence of prison, the crowded conditions of the ghetto, or the unloving effects of racism on a daily basis, we need someone who has been where we are and who has lived to tell about it.

Where can we find such a guide? Who can be trusted to show us the way past prison rape, ghetto violence, and other threatening situations? History is full of self-styled messiahs, such as David Koresh and Jim Jones, claiming to bring healing and protection to scarred, damaged lives. Indeed, opportunists have been setting up and preying on innocents since the beginning of time.

Identity of False Prophets. How can the vulnerable discern who are true prophets and who are merely perpetrating or pretending? What distinguishing marks do they have? What do they look like? The answer is simple. True prophets receive their messages from the God of the Bible, whereas false prophets do not. The issue, according to Cambridge graduate and noted Bible scholar Leon J. Wood, is not whether a prophet only thought he heard from the God of the Bible but whether he really did have communications from heaven (Wood, 109). Did the God of the Bible, in fact, tell the leader of Jonestown to serve the cyanide punch that resulted in mass suicide? Did the God of the Bible tell Koresh to torch his flock?

Prophet Mohammed, Wallace Fard, Elijah Muhammad, Louis Farrakhan, and Jesus Christ all claim to represent the true God of the Bible, insisting they have been called to deliver the people from their present hardships via Islam or Christianity respectively. It is up to twenty-eight million Black Americans to discern which claims are true and which are false. Biblical scholars use the following eight objective signs to distinguish between true and false prophets. Understanding these signs will be most helpful in avoiding seduction by another lying prophet or blind guide.

Discerning the Prophets

Divination Not Employed	Harmony of the Message
Character of the Message	Fulfillment of Prophecy
Character of the Prophet	Authentication by Miracles
Willingness to Suffer	Spiritual Discernment

Divination Not Employed. A clear sign to use in discerning the veracity of a prophet is whether or not he uses divination. By that we mean reading or interpreting signs or visions that cause one to see into the future. For example, Louis Farrakhan claims to have experienced the vision in Ezekiel 1 regarding the wheels and four creatures. He maintains that this is, in fact, a UFO hovering forty miles above the earth, which follows him day and night.

The pilot is none other than Elijah Muhammad, back from the dead. It seems Muhammad was also the design engineer for this aircraft that will one day destroy the world. Meanwhile, Muhammad and the millions of Black souls aboard the UFO peer out the bay windows and watch Minister Farrakhan's every move. According to Farrakhan's vision, this machine is not powered by imagination but by Allah, which is in fact a name for a seventh-century moon god (Hanagraph).

It must be pointed out that Minister Farrakhan has gone far beyond the teachings of his predecessors, Fard and Muhammad, by using not only the Quran but the Bible as well to revise earlier Black Muslim teachings into his own unique doctrine. In fact, Farrakhan quotes from the Bible far more than he quotes from the Quran. (See the appendix for a sample of the numerous biblical references Minister Farrakhan borrows and misuses.) His sermons are so filled with Bible imagery that it sounds almost as if he is inside a Christian church rather than in a mosque (Morey, 169). However, it is his interpretation of these images and Scripture with which we beg to differ.

According to rules of evidence, since Farrakhan introduced the Bible in support of his doctrines, we are free to cross-examine any inconsistencies. Again, the goal is to discern who in fact represents the God of the Bible. The vision described in Ezekiel 1 has more to do with the glory of the God of the Bible than with the glory of Farrakhan or Muhammad. Israel had departed from the God of the Bible and was experiencing hardship. Much like many Black Americans today, they were captive socially, economically, and spiritually.

Ezekiel's vision represents a holy, all-powerful, all-knowing God of the Bible who has seen, and continues to see, all the oppression experienced by humankind. God's deliverance from hellish situations comes through the man seated on the throne, Jesus Christ, not through Farrakhan or Muhammad. It is Jesus who is the supreme revelation of the God of the Bible, chosen to restore order to this world of disorder. Moreover, the vision stresses the holiness of the God of the Bible as not being a quality that He has but, rather, His very essence.

He is totally separate from man. He does not think or function like man. He hates sin even if it is in response to someone who has sinned against you. And yet Farrakhan teaches that the God of the Bible is merely a man of flesh and blood and not, as he says, a "spook."

According to Leon Wood, "The hallmark of a true prophet is that he possesses a sense of awe and holy fear of God. While the false prophet chatters glibly about God because he has never met Him, the true messenger of God leaves His presence indelibly marked with the glory of His Lord and His holiness" (Wood, 109).

Character of the Message. False prophets usually speak messages that the people *want* to hear whereas true prophets tell the people what they *need* to hear. Minister Farrakhan asserts that a race of devils was created by the evil Mr. Yacub, enemy of Allah. These devils are the White European race and are the sole people responsible for misleading nine-tenths of the population of the Black nation (Muhammad, 68).

Minister Farrakhan also incites his captive audience with tales of Jewish exploitation of Black Americans:

> *They didn't apologize for putting my brothers and sisters to live in homes and apartments and charging them the highest rents, nor setting up liquor stores when they don't drink too much themselves, nor seducing a young girl (Vannessa Williams) to take her clothes off. . . . We've been loyal to (them). We've cleaned (their) floors and nursed (their) children. We give (them) our talent and (they) manage us. (They) get the money, we get the fame and then end up on drugs with no money.* (Karrupa [author's parentheses], 20)

Jesus Christ, on the other hand, told the people – be they Jew, Gentile, slave, or free – that it was up to each individual to clean up his act, to repent. His message so

incensed the religious leaders of that day that they con-
spired to have Jesus crucified. Apparently, calling them
phonies – outwardly religious but inwardly wicked – did
not win Jesus many friends but rather influenced His
enemies to unite in opposition to Him. Nonetheless,
Jesus boldly stated, "I am the way, the truth, and the
life; no man comes to the Father but through me" (John
14:6 NASB).

Character of the Prophet. Examining a prophet's
background is an excellent way to discover who is of the
God of the Bible and who is of man. This discovery
process will unearth all sorts of clues into the model's
positive and negative character patterns.

Consider the issue of polygamy, for example.
According to the Quran, this tradition of having more
than one wife is legitimate. Although Farrakhan – the
latest guide for the Nation of Islam – has only one wife,
his predecessors, Prophet Mohammed and Elijah
Muhammad (whom he claims are God incarnate), had
many wives (Morey, 99). In fact, Mohammed *miracu-
lously* had a convenient revelation from Allah when he
decided to take for himself the wife of his adopted son
Zaid. Talk about indecent proposals!

If the leader abuses his immediate family, what is to
stop him from damaging his followers with lies and dis-
tortions of truth to suit his own purposes? Consequently,
it is vitally important to discern a model's integrity,
thereby avoiding future consequences of yet another
damaging relationship. False prophets are infamous for
deceiving, lying, and pretending to be what they are not.
For instance, Farrakhan claims to have healed the sick
although there exists no independent documentation of
that. There is, on the other hand, extensive
documentation of Jesus' healing a demoniac, cleansing
a leper, healing an impotent, raising Lazarus from the

dead, to say nothing of His own resurrection from the dead, an event that alone had 500 eyewitness reports (McDowell, 224; Matthew 8:3; Luke 4:35; John 5:5; 11:43).

Another character point to ponder centers on the 1991 Savior's Day celebration in which Minister Farrakhan was introduced as wonderful, counselor, mighty God, the everlasting father, the prince of peace. This is the same introduction that Isaiah gives to Jesus Christ 700 years before His birth (Isaiah 7:14)! What is noteworthy is that whereas both are called the prince of peace, Minister Farrakhan makes no apologies for his incessant verbal attacks on White devils and Jews. Jesus, on the other hand, preached reconciliation and by His death tore down the things that separate us and make us enemies – e.g., money, race, and class (Ephesians 2:15-16).

And yet Minister Farrakhan would have Black Americans follow a religion whose founder made a clear distinction with respect to racial class. In *Hadith* 66, a companion to the Quran, Mohammed refers to Blacks not only as slaves but also as "raisin heads." He goes on to say that it is an abomination for a Muslim to even dream of a Black woman. Have not Black Americans been verbally abused enough with second-class citizenship and derogatory terms such as kaffir boy and nigger? Should we follow a leader whose religion is founded in racism and low esteem for our ethnicity?

Jesus, on the other hand, loved "hanging" with the outcast, the reject, the indigent. When He was thirsty, it was a Samaritan (whom people regarded with contempt) with whom He spent the afternoon in affirming conversation (John 4). And she was a woman at that! That was quite a radical statement in those days – perhaps even today in the vortex of the Afro-Asian world.

On other occasions, it was publicans and sinners with whom Jesus reclined, much to the chagrin of the religiously conservative Pharisees (Matthew 9:10-11). And it was on the tortuous road to Calvary's brow, with a Black man named Simon the Cyrene, that Jesus spent some of His last hours on earth. To Jesus, there was neither bondservant nor free, elite nor poor. Everyone, no matter how different, could become united through entering a personal relationship with Him.

Willingness to Suffer. Though no one likes to suffer, a true prophet will endure hardship for the sake of his message. False prophets, however, are not willing to do this, desiring an easy life. If they do suffer, they take everybody with them, as in the cases of James Jones and David Koresh.

Consider Minister Farrakhan, who while preaching separation from Jews and White devils, elects to reside in the fashionable, partially Jewish Hyde Park district of Chicago.

Perhaps this choice of a home base is strategic, having more to do with a desire to shed his antagonistic image and reach a larger integrated base. According to a recent article, Minister Farrakhan believes that repairing relations with Jews will make it more acceptable for influential Blacks to associate with him. Nonetheless, instead of facing the music concerning the pain his anti-semitic criticisms have caused, Farrakhan simply plays concertos (*Newsweek*, 31).

Jesus, on the other hand, predicted His death and resurrection to the disciples, going so far as to say that one of His own disciples would betray Him (Matthew 16:21). And yet He still offered forgiveness and mercy to Judas even after "homey" sold Him out for thirty pieces of silver.

Harmony of the Message. A true prophet's messages harmonize with the law of the God of the Bible and with the message of other prophets of God. In essence, they all sing off the same song sheet.

For example, Farrakhan denies the virgin birth of Jesus, asserting that the Holy Spirit who came upon Mary and impregnated her was the spirit of a man and not a spook. On the other hand, Isaiah, Matthew, Luke, and others attest to the virgin birth. In Isaiah 7:14, the prophet says that a virgin shall conceive and shall bear a son and shall call His name Immanuel.

Moreover, in the first chapter of Luke, Mary is assured that she, a virgin, would conceive. "How shall this be," said Mary, "seeing I know not a man?" The angel answered that the power of the highest would overshadow her and the "holy thing which shall be born of thee shall be called the Son of God" (Luke 1:34-35).

When Joseph finds out that his fiancee is pregnant, an angel warns him not to leave her, for that which was in her womb was of the Holy Ghost (Matthew 1:20-21). This is no harder to believe than that in the beginning the God of the Bible created man from the earth and woman from man's rib. Long before invitro fertilization and artificial insemination, the God of the Bible was in the baby-making business.

Fulfillment of Predictive Prophecy. True prophets batted 1.000 whereas false prophets went zero for four. Take, for example, the talk concerning the mysterious UFO wheel that tails Minister Farrakhan. According to his mentor, Elijah Muhammad, the year 1914 signaled the end of the White devil's rule on earth. Muhammad went on to prophesy that White control would end in 1975 and that Black Americans would rule the world. He cited the vision of the wheels in Ezekiel as the reference for this decisive battle (Muhammad, 290).

Needless to say, this did not happen. The major power shift in 1975 was toward the Middle East as its oil cartel (OPEC) continued to flex its recently acquired muscle, increasing the financial stress of Black Americans as well as the anguish of all Americans.

Minister Farrakhan himself got into the prognostications ball game by predicting a race war for 1986. On March 11, 1984, he said, "Some of the White people will survive this war but God does not want them living with us." "Make no mistake," he went on to say, "We are going to shake the world and the Jews are especially frightened, because they have an idea of what is rolling around in the back of my brain" (Kramer, 17). But, again, this prediction did not come to pass.

On the other hand, the Old Testament predicted the coming of Jesus in Genesis 3:15 and the time of that advent in Genesis 49:10. His divinity was prophesied many times in the Old Testament (Psalms 2:7-11; 45:6-11; Isaiah 9:6; Jeremiah 23:6; Micah 5:2). These prophecies have been fulfilled.

In addition, Christ's mission, miracles, persecution, triumphant entry into Jerusalem, betrayal by a friend for thirty pieces of silver, desertion by His disciples, false accusations against His character, patience under suffering, death in the prime of His life, death with thieves, bones not broken, His resurrection, and His ascension into heaven were all foretold and fulfilled (McDowell, 175-176).

It is worth mentioning that though Jesus' disciples did not take prophecies of His death, burial, and resurrection very seriously, His enemies did. Following the illegal hearings implicating Jesus, the scribes and Pharisees took great pains to make sure that an armed guard stood at the tomb to keep Jesus from leaving. When that failed, they concocted the story that the disciples had stolen His body. The truth is that the resurrected Jesus was seen by more than 500 individuals after His death (McDowell, 224).

Interestingly enough false prophecy has also been fulfilled time and again throughout history. The diabolic power of Satan is able to provide some authentication for his false prophecies. Satan and his prophets cannot, however, stand against the one true God of the Bible. In spite of that, necromancers claiming to have the spirit of the God of the Bible consistently utilize any advantage to lead people toward idol worship.

In Deuteronomy 18, Moses instructs the children of Israel not to follow an enchanter, diviner, observer of times, or a charmer. Perhaps Minister Farrakhan, who was called "the charmer" during His calypso band years, is the fulfillment of prophecy after all!

Authentication by Miracles. The sign of miracles is not conclusive evidence of "the real thing" because false prophets can also perform miracles beyond human ability. Their source of power is Satan, who follows them around showing signs and doing lying wonders. Mark warns, "False Christs and false prophets will arise, and will show signs and wonders, in order, if possible, to lead even the elect astray" (Mark 13:22 NASB). Further, the people were told that any prophet who tried to get them to follow after other gods was false and that they should not follow such a one (Deuteronomy 13:1-3).

Minister Farrakhan asserts that not only is he the manifestation of God but so were Elijah Muhammad and Wallace Fard. In his *Message to the Black Man in America,* one of the Nation of Islam's primary study tools, the statement is made that God must be a man and not a spook. This reasoning comes from Habakkuk's vision of God coming from the sons of man (Muhammad, 7). *Message to the Black Man in America* goes on to instruct Black Americans to ditch the God of their fathers and follow the seventh-century moon god Allah and his 360 idols, whom they do not know!

It is interesting to note that Minister Farrakhan calls for a separate nation for Black Americans. He wants millions of Blacks to relocate to Africa where they have limited skills and opportunities. What is unclear is how these Black Americans will fare in a country such as Kenya, where we were told by a villager in Nyahruru that the average wage is less than $20 a month. Minister Farrakhan "wants us to ask our African brothers and sisters, already beset by economic, medical and social hardships, to set aside land to build a separate and independent nation, financed by American dollars currently spent to keep Black Americans incarcerated" (Mills, 114).

It is more than coincidental that David Koresh and Jim Jones also felt that isolation at Ranch Apocalypse and Jonestown, respectively, was the best thing for their followers. This move from the larger society and its problems proved fatal in each case. Our Creator knew that following false gods could be hazardous to one's health.

Spiritual Discernment. What is your gut reaction when you encounter a prophet? Listen to your heart. The Scriptures assert that sheep know their shepherd, but a stranger they will not follow (John 10:27-29). It is only the person who is far from the God of the Bible Himself who is in danger of becoming, as Morey puts it, "Farra-conned."

In Ezekiel 34:1-6, the prophet says that a false shepherd would not feed his flock but rather eat their food, take their money, and clothe himself. It is a documented fact that Minister Farrakhan's Power Products (an economic incentive program for building the Nation) have garnered little for the Black Muslim peddler of these self-help products. Instead, these bean pie, newspaper, restaurant, and fish ventures are said to rely on the super exploitation of members' labor, based on low-wage employment with little or no benefits (Reed, 54).

While he resides in his palatial estate surrounded by an eight-foot fence, in an upwardly mobile neighborhood, his followers languish in urban ghettos surrounded by red lines and other invisible fences. And whatever became of the $5 million dollar interest-free loan given to Minister Farrakhan by Qaddafi?

Jesus, on the other hand, is the true shepherd, laying down His life for His followers. He did not spend more than $50,000, as did Minister Farrakhan, to speak at Madison Square Garden in order to recruit middle class proselytes. Everything Jesus had He gave away, including His life. Nonetheless, a natural man, as the apostle Paul noted, would not be able to discern such things and would count it foolishness. Paying more attention to the quick fix of rehabbing a drug-infested apartment complex in Washington and anti-crime patrols in New York, Chicago, Detroit, and Atlanta, followers are charmed into embracing a seventh-century Bedouin existence.

Did not Jim Jones clean up the neighborhoods in urban Indianapolis? Did not David Koresh provide food and safe housing for his followers in Waco? Of course they did . . . temporarily, that is. Then all chaos broke lose. Cyanide was swallowed, kerosene was poured, and lives were lost forever.

Jesus did not come to kill but to deliver us. He came not that we would have death, but life – and that more abundantly. He knew that our problem was not skin, but sin. He alone went to the cross to deliver humankind and reconcile persons to each other and to the God of the Bible. Although He had no intentions of convincing His followers that they had to physically die with Him, He did insist that they put to death their old way of living, hating, and thinking toward themselves and their neighbors.

To attain a quality of eternal life, a life of unbroken fellowship with the God of the Bible, a peace in the midst of daily storms, we need not only (1) a map that is precise, (2) a model that is pure and trustworthy, but also (3) a method that is practical. The acquisition of such a life will be explored in chapter 3.

3

A Method That Is Practical

Sirs, what must I do to be saved?
Acts 16:30

What would you do if someone you loved were in danger of losing his or her life? No doubt, you would either rush to his aid or seek the assistance of a trained professional who could offer hope to your desperate situation. That is exactly what Reba and Chip McClure did one fall afternoon when their newlywed bliss turned into a living nightmare.

On a chilly day in October 1987, these young parents, along with millions of Americans, nervously hoped against hope for the rescue of their eighteen-month-old Jessica who had fallen down an uncapped well in her aunt's backyard in Midland, Texas. Because the well was only eight inches in diameter, rescuers could not blast their way to the trapped toddler without seriously injuring her legs, showering her in debris, and jeopardizing her chances for survival.

As hope began to fade, volunteers dug a new "well" next to the existing one. The new shaft intercepted the existing one. Then they dug a tunnel upward to the toddler nicknamed "Juicy," whose tiny body was wedged in the narrow shaft twenty-two feet from the surface. Two and one-half days later, these heroic measures saved little Jessica and returned her to the arms of her grateful parents. Had it not been for the excavation methods of these intrepid people, the toddler would have surely perished. Indeed, thousands if not millions are rescued from harm, danger, or a loss because of lifesaving efforts of someone who knows what to do.

Whether it's a medical, financial, legal, or personal emergency, the ability to make the right decision can make all the difference between success and failure. Hence, we rely on doctors, lawyers, paramedics, accountants, and pastors to provide the correct technical procedures to save our lives, our fortunes, and our families. For instance, when a person quits breathing, there are definite steps to follow for restoring air to the lungs. According to *Dorland's Illustrated Medical Journal,* proper understanding of cardiopulmonary resuscitation (CPR) can make the difference between life and death:

1. Clear the victim's mouth and throat of any obstruction.
2. Tilt the head backwards.
3. Insert your thumb between the victim's teeth while keeping the head pushed back.
4. Pinch his nostrils shut.
5. Take a deep breath and blow forcefully into the victim's mouth.

Now, let's apply this analogy to religion. There are certain religious procedures by which someone can be "saved." Saved from what? The danger of being eternally separated from the God of the Bible – the peril of being forever cut off from hope.

Although there exist alternative procedures that are reputed to procure such salvation, we must ask if they are, like CPR, the preferred method. Will they revive your marriage in this life and sustain your soul in the next? Can they bring the sex addict, drunkard, or incest victim back from a life of shame to a life of respect?

With millions of Black Americans wanting rescue from their hell on earth, time is of the essence. Just as you have only minutes to administer CPR before brain damage or death occurs, many marriages, families, and lives are hanging in the balance even now. They need salvation today. They cannot depend on an alternative method that could leave them impaired for life, a method that may cause further damage to, say, the prison rape victim's already diminished sense of self-worth. Consider the following example.

Suppose you have been told to use a finger probe to help save a choking victim's life. You methodically feel around the *outside* of his throat, probing for reasons as to why this person is gagging. However, minutes pass by and he collapses.

"What happened," you wonder? Well, a finger probe is something you do *inside* a victim's mouth, and then only if you see the object. Yes, you thought you were "saving" his life but your redefinition of the "finger probe" method did more harm than good. Semantics, then, the study of the true meaning of words, is vital. What you think will revive your marriage could put you in the divorce court. What you hope will protect you from prison rape could ultimately violate your soul.

Therefore, we need to clearly define our terminology when discussing salvation. Walter Martin, a foremost scholar in the area of cults, has this to say concerning terminology and language:

> *Language to be sure is a complex subject. But one thing is beyond dispute, and that is, in context, words mean just what they say. Either we admit this or we surrender all the accomplishments of grammar and scholastic progress, and return to writing on cave walls with charcoal sticks.* (Martin, 21)

Martin adds that redefining terms is an absurdity:

> *For example, a doctor who says he is going to perform open heart surgery and proceeds to take out your gall bladder in the presence of his colleagues, then defends his actions with the flimsy excuse that open heart surgery really means gall bladder removal, would not be in the medical profession very long.* (Martin, 22)

No legitimate profession tolerates this kind of confusion of terminology. Religion can be no different. Believing you are "saved" but using a double meaning could put you in danger. What then must twenty-eight million Blacks do to be saved from their hellish existence? Christianity has a methodology, and so does the Nation of Islam. But which one is most practical? Which is the God of the Bible's preferred method? Let's compare.

Five Pillars. According to the Quran, the method of salvation involves strict adherence to five pillars of faith:

1. Recitation of the Shahadah: "There is no god but Allah, and Mohammed is the prophet of Allah."
2. Five daily prayers — before sunrise, at noon, afternoon, sunset, and at night. This includes lying prostrate facing the holy city of Mecca.

3. Almsgiving (giving one-fortieth of your income to charitable causes).

4. Fasting during the entire month of Ramadan (between dawn and sunset) that lasts twenty-seven to twenty-eight days from the sighting of one new moon to the next. It entails daytime abstinence from all food and drink for atonement for one's sins during the previous year.

5. Pilgrimage to Mecca, the holy city, at least once in a Muslim's lifetime.

Every Black Muslim who practices these five pillars hopes to escape the judgment of Allah. Each pillar, however, raises serious questions, as we will discover. Again, we wish not to offend but to enlighten.

Recitation of the Shahadah. Before you recite the Shahadah honoring Allah's holiness, you need to know what the term *Allah* really means. In pre-Islamic history, Allah was a well-known name referring not to a supreme god but to a pagan seventh-century moon deity. According to Islamic scholars, the *Muslim World Journal*, the *Encyclopedia of Islam*, and the *Encyclopedia of Religion*, Arabs worshiped this Meccan deity who appeared in pre-Islamic poetry and in Arabic inscriptions as husband of a sun goddess (Morey, 48-51).

Now, Muhammad and Farrakhan hold that Allah is God. But which Allah is able to save your soul? The pagan moon deity used by an astral religion in pre-Islamic Arabia or the redefined god of Islam?

Five Daily Prayers. Suppose you are a Black Muslim incarcerated in the state penitentiary. What happens if you have kitchen detail and miss a prayer? Is it too late to say your prayers after KP?

In fact, there are some interesting limitations to what prayers this transcendent god will and will not hear. In

Hadith 66, it is said that if you pass gas or have bad breath, Allah will not hear your prayers. Is this fair? Should you keep Pepto Bismol and Scope on hand at times of prayer? Since twenty-eight million Blacks are being asked to depend on these prayers, this is a very serious issue.

Another point to ponder is an interesting requirement found in the *Book of Wisdom to the Elders of Islam.* Both parents of a newborn must be on site to recite the Adhaan and Iqaamah prayers at the moment of birth along with certain prayers for the protection of the child from the devil. If not, the child's force field will be broken and can never be mended. Suppose the father has to work or is in jail when the mom goes into labor? Will the child then go to hell? Is there no salvation? (Al Haadi, 154).

Of course, there are other prayers that a father, mother, or other Black Muslim can recite for extra credit. For example, by reciting "Glory to thee Allah, and praise to him, glory to Allah the great" one hundred times, one's sins will be forgiven even though they may be countless (Al Haadi, 184). But what happens if you only recite it ninety-nine times? Do you have to start over at the beginning? Are those ninety-nine prayers wasted?

One more thing. Praying toward Mecca is, in fact, a practice growing out of the seventh-century that involves idol worship of Allah, the moon god of the Kabah. The entire fertile crescent participated in this astral time of intercession. The pagan ritual prescribed praying in the direction of Mecca because their gods were thought to be conveniently located there (Morey, 52).

Almsgiving. With thousands of Black men and women incarcerated and thousands more unemployed, how practical is it to require financial contributions as a condition of salvation? They can barely earn enough to pay the gas bill, the phone bill, or even the rent, much less earn their way to heaven through almsgiving no matter how meager. Moreover, even if you have good intentions to render unto Allah what is due Allah, what happens if you forget? Does Allah then say, "Go to hell"?

Fasting. Suppose it's your birthday and your homeys take you out for baby back ribs. Should you abstain while everyone else eats, drinks, and gets merry? What about the family whose children are already undernourished? When dad gets his overtime check on Ramadan, should the kids go hungry in order to save their souls? Fasting is a good practice. It may cleanse the body, but should it be a prerequisite to individual salvation?

Besides, if Allah and the God of the Bible were the same, consider that the prophet Isaiah says that the God of the Bible is weary of fasts (Isaiah 58). Did He not require internal abstinence in preference to external displays? In fact, the Bible warns against being outwardly righteous (such as praying, fasting, and giving alms) while being inwardly wicked (Matthew 23). It appears that these practices have been tried before and judged unacceptable by the God of the Bible. If He rejected these outward signs before, will He not do the same again?

Pilgrimage to Mecca. What if you can't afford the trip? If you have been laid off your job and do not have $2,000 or more in discretionary income to purchase a round-trip ticket even at the super-saver rate, is there a waiver because you cannot afford this pilgrimage? If, in fact, as both Muslim and Western scholars note, the Kabah is a stone temple of more than 360 idols that represent deities for everyone, why then would you consider making a pilgrimage to this pagan cult center anyway? Is this another redefinition? Has Allah now got good religion?

What Is the Conclusion? If the truth were told, I would venture to say that there is not one Black Muslim who has kept all five pillars his entire life. So the question arises, are their methods of salvation, their pillars of faith, really do-able? If you were to die today, Black Muslim, could you be assured of salvation?

There is more. According to the Quran, there is an addendum to these pillars. One's deeds will be considered in the equation. But is there anyone whose righteous deeds outweigh your bad deeds? Does not the Bible teach that there is none righteous? All have sinned and fallen short of the glory of the God of the Bible (Romans 3:23).

Yet, according to the Black Muslims, this is a misinterpretation. They say it really does not mean sin as we know it in the Western world. But as we established in chapter 1, the Quran is to give way in terms of authenticity to the older document, the Bible. Therefore, according to Isaiah 64:6, all of our righteous acts are as filthy rags.

Even Prophet Mohammed had sin in his life. He needed forgiveness (Sura 18:110). If this incarnation of Christ (according to Minister Farrakhan) needed forgiveness, what about the average Black Muslim? When his life is weighed in the balance, will he be found wanting? This is no misnomer. Sin is real. Hell is real. And yet, if you depend on some alternate terminology to escape your hellish existence, you could lose your life in both this world *and* the next.

Double Entendre. In the Black Muslim booklet, *Where is Hell,* hell is defined as whatever you make it in this world, plus there is a second chance to clean up your act before reaching Allah in the next. Fire and brimstone are redefined as burning passion residing in the hearts and bosoms of humankind (Al Haadi, 177).

The question is often asked about the size of hell. Again Black Muslims are told that hell is however big your minds make it. Discipline is played up, and a voracious, ravenous craving in one's body and mind is played down.

This kind of talk can be appealing to prison inmates, many of whom learn the art of denial of basic needs, such as food, simply to avoid the discomfort of feeling the need. After being incarcerated for several years, these God-given desires for peach cobbler and relationships come to be regarded with contempt. In a desperate attempt at survival, remarkably reminiscent of Aesop's "sour grapes" fable, many inmates discipline themselves not to want, not to eat, not to trust — especially "White devils"! Is this practical?

Allender maintains that a self-imposed hatred of any of our God-given longings is no less that a clenched fist that says to the God of the Bible, "Why did *You* make me want relationships and then isolate me in a twelve-by-twenty-foot cell? Why did *You* put in me the desire to make a significant impact in my neighborhood, on my job, and in my family when the "system" puts so many obstacles in my way? Why did *You* make *me* desire beef rib tips when all *I* get is day-old carrots and meat filler?" The problem is not our desires so much as our need to discipline our wants.

For instance, the God of the Bible intended that relationships demonstrate cooperation, that people can get along regardless of differences in race, age, or gender. In this context, strange as it may seem, the absence of relationships can be viewed as a gift from the God of the Bible.

Here's how. According to Allender, loneliness gives us a picture of hell, of what it means to be eternally isolated from the God of the Bible and other people. It also makes us agree with God that it is not good for man to be alone. It helps us comprehend how dependent we are on the God of the Bible to make our relationships work. When we trivialize His purpose for relationships, however, we may seek quick relief. We may join the Nation of Islam or, perhaps, become too dependent on other people. On the other hand, sometimes the opposite happens: we push people away altogether.

The question may be framed in this way: *Is the Nation of Islam's disciplined, rigid view of relationships between men and women as well as between Blacks and Whites simply a quick fix for convicted rapists* (such as Mike Tyson, now known as Malik Abdul Aziz) *who need to feel vindicated, who need to have dignity restored, and who need to enjoy a decent relationship with females?*

Will Aziz fare better under the training of Minister Farrakhan than he did under the eye of Don King? Or will this salvation method promote external changes while ignoring his internal problems in dealing with people? After all, wasn't it Aziz's attitude toward women that put him in prison in the first place?

Yes, the God of the Bible created us to be involved in something bigger than ourselves, bigger than being heavyweight champion of the world. But that desire is to be satisfied legitimately, not through beating up and man-handling female counterparts who may foolishly follow the hawk into the chicken coop, as Minister Farrakhan puts it (Tyson Documentary, 1993)!

It is not the desire for companionship that is wrong. What is wrong is the clenched fist that says, "I'll make women submit to me my own way. I'll come up with an alternative solution for my personal anger and isolation problems. I don't need the God of the Bible. If that fails, I will turn to Farrakhan to give me a sense of being accepted for who I am, clenched fist and all."

We live in a fallen world where sin abounds. Therefore, we cannot escape the fact of our depravity. Yet the Black Muslims will redefine salvation as Five Pillars and hell as whatever your mind will make it. For Malik Abdul Aziz, then, hell might simply mean spending another lonely weekend in solitary confinement or having more and more time away from people added to his six-year prison term. Again, this is redefining biblical terminology. Hell is a real place with fire and brimstone that is not for purification but for eternal separation and eternal torment (Revelation 21:8). There is a great gulf fixed where no one can cross over and receive a second chance (Luke 16:26).

According to Walter Martin, to spiritualize texts and doctrines (such as salvation and hell) or to attempt to explain them away on the basis of the nebulous term "interpretation" is scholastic dishonesty and is commonly found in cult literature. Thus, salvation becomes a five-pillar approach, hell becomes what you make it with a second chance to do things better, and millions of Blacks such as Malik Aziz are led astray. With our desires, wants, and needs at stake, can we really afford to buy into this methodology for salvation?

One Pillar. By contrast, the Christian methodology for salvation is founded on one rock, one pillar — Jesus Christ. There is no other name under heaven whereby we can be saved (Acts 4:12). Peter adds that the stone, Christ, that people rejected is the chief pillar for Christianity (1 Peter 2:7).

Before Christ, fasts were kept, prayers made, alms given, and belief in the God of the Bible was recognized. But these laws, ceremonies, and rituals were simply the schoolmaster to teach everyone that they had indeed sinned (Galatians 3:24). Furthermore, the law shows us our need for a savior (Romans 7). The things we want to do (not covet, not commit adultery, not rape) we do because of our fallen nature.

Yet, Jesus came and lived a sinless life, accomplishing what we could not do. He was the sacrifice, the Lamb that took away the sins of the world. Therefore, there remains no more sacrifice, almsgiving, daily prayers, feasts, and fasts to be given. They were only a shadow of the real thing. And once He sat down at the Father's right hand after Calvary, there was nothing more to be done. "It is finished," He announced (John 20:30).

According to the Bible, we are sanctified (set apart from sin) through the offering of Jesus Christ's body once and for all (Hebrews 10:10) But if we reject this truth, we are out of luck. There is no more sacrifice for our sins to save us from this hellish existence on earth and the hell hole we will inhabit for all eternity.

Alms won't cut it. Prayers can't do the trick. A trip to Mecca is not sufficient. Only a fearful looking toward judgment is our doom. And as the epistle to the Hebrew church notes, it is a fearful thing to fall into the hands of the living the God of the Bible (Hebrews 10:31). But that does not have to happen. You can receive the free gift of salvation in three steps: *repent, confess, and believe!*

Repent. The Bible says our very nature is anti-God. From the first act of disobedience in the Garden of Eden to this very day, we exercise our God-given free will to do our own thing. Nonetheless, if we repent – that is, if we have a change of heart about how truly messed up we really are – we will find mercy. We will receive help.

Luke 18 describes an interesting parable about a tax collector and a Pharisee. This could easily have been about a Christian and a Muslim. When both went up to the church (or Mosque) and prayed, one justified himself while the other humbled himself.

For analogy's sake, the Pharisee's prayer might be paraphrased as follows:

Lord, I thank thee that I am not like other men, especially White devils who are robbers and exploiters of our Black women – or even like this miserable Christian. I fast during Ramadan, pray in Arabic seven times daily, fly to Mecca once a year, and give alms to ghetto youth.

But the poor Christian stood far off and prayed simply, "Lord, forgive me, a sinner." Jesus said that the humbled person who recognized his sin and that he could never work, fast, or pray his way to salvation went away more justified than the devout religious person. Everyone who exalts himself will be humbled, and he who humbles himself will be exalted (Luke 18:9-14).

Indeed, it is humbling to rely solely on the finished work of Jesus Christ's death and resurrection and not on our own good works. Yet, as Paul told another community heavy into pagan deities and astral religions, it is by grace that we are saved through faith, and we had nothing to do with it. Salvation is a gift of the God of the Bible, lest anyone boast about how many prayers they recited and how many trips they made to the city of Mecca (Ephesians 2:8-9). Once you realize the true condition of your soul, take the next step and tell the truth.

Confess. A person can know that he or she is an alcoholic or a sex addict and never tell a soul. Confession is humbling. It is agreeing with the God of the Bible about the real you, the one nobody knows. It is telling the truth on yourself – pointing the finger, not at the White devil or the person who turned you in, but at the man in the mirror.

The apostle Paul, after citing the God of the Bible's open-and-shut case against humankind in the first nine chapters of Romans, gives us some good news. We can, "cop a plea," as it were. We can receive immunity if we confess with our mouth the Lord Jesus Christ (not Allah or Farrakhan) and believe in our hearts that the God of the Bible has raised Christ (not the prophet of al-Islam) from the dead. Then God's charges against us will be dropped (Romans 10:9-10). It's that simple. Although Black Muslims hold that "Christianity is a welfare religion, Jesus paid it all, and Black folk need to earn their salvation," the method remains the same (Guthrie, 40).

Believe. "Nothing can be that easy," you say. "My whole life has been one difficulty after another, from my foster-home upbringing to being found guilty of a crime I didn't commit to my unmerciful White devil parole officer. Now you say, 'Simply believe' and I can be saved?"

Well, not just believe. James says that even the devils believe and tremble (James 2:19). Farrakhan believes. The point, dear reader, is that "what" you believe makes all the difference.

Believe on the Lord Jesus Christ – the anointed one, according to the Quran. Believe that the God of the Bible raised Him from the dead. Five hundred eyewitnesses attest to that fact no matter how much the Quran, Farrakhan, and the Black Muslims deny it.

Even King Agrippa confided in Paul that he was almost persuaded to be a Christian (Acts 26:28). But "almost" is not good enough. You must confess Him with your mouth and believe in your heart. Then you shall be saved.

When Jesus died He provided a practical means of salvation for young, old, rich, and poor alike that could be experienced on a daily basis as well as throughout eternity. And yet *Message to the Black man in America,* the pocket companion for new Muslim proselytes, teaches something entirely different about eternity and the hereafter:

> *Read the Scriptures carefully on the life in the hereafter, and try to understand it; you will find that it does not actually mean what you have been believing. No one is going to leave this planet and live on another. You can't – even if you try. You can't reach the moon if you try; so be satisfied and believe in Allah while you are on this good earth but be righteous.* (Muhammad, 305)

Moreover, Muhammad, Farrakhan, and their Black Muslim followers also believe:

- That the White devils made up the pie-in-the-sky story to inhibit Blacks from getting the slice that they owe you here on earth.

- That your portion will come from the bean pie economic plan on earth under the ministration of Louis Farrakhan.

- That Black women should be protected from the "Paleman" who is destroying Black families through careers and women's liberation and, therefore, controlling Black men (Al Haadi, 121).

- In the veracity of the Bible, but that it has been tampered with.

- Judgment will first take place in America.

- The evil Dr. Yacub brought into the world the White devils who are giving you so much hell on earth.

- Allah appeared in the person of Wallace Fard in July 1930 and is the long-awaited Mahdi of Muslims and the Messiah of Christians (Muhammad, 161).

- Muhammad is the Christ and Farrakhan is the fulfillment of Isaiah 9:6, the child who would be the prince of peace (Hanagraph).

What you believe determines your behavior. How you behave determines your quality of life. For example, Malik Aziz believed that he was going out for a night on the town, but instead, ended up in a very undesirable Indiana correctional facility.

No matter how the deck is stacked, each person, according to the prophet Ezekiel, is liable for his or her own belief system and for the truths they embrace (Ezekiel 18). When it is all said and done, whether you receive the God of the Bible's gift of salvation through Jesus Christ or harden your heart, the Bible, the older document, says that people shall know that a prophet has been among them.

If you believe that the God of the Bible has raised Christ from the dead, a fact that, again, was substantiated by 500 eyewitnesses, you can enter a personal and public relationship with the Lord Jesus Christ in this life and the next. What does this mean? Let me explain.

Personal Salvation. The God of the Bible is interested in every individual, including Malik Aziz and Haman Cross, being freed from the everyday hellish existence of sex addiction, anger, or the desire to fight back when abused by women. This individual salvation frees me from blame shifting for meeting my innermost desires.

It frees me from hating the judge who sentenced me. It frees me from roaming the streets (prowling) for precious life and one-night stands. No matter what the law says I am guilty of, the God of the Bible declares me innocent before Him; and we take our failures one day at a time from that point. When I get angry, behave irresponsibly, and end up in solitary confinement, I repent, not to get saved again but to maintain unbroken fellowship with the God of the Bible. That is what eternal life is, an unbroken relationship with the Creator. It's that easy. When Jesus died, it was so that Malik, I, and everyone else would have a practical, personal means of salvation. But salvation also deals with public issues.

Public Salvation. Justice is the Christian mandate for public salvation as it relates to politics. Fairness is the mandate as it relates to our social lives. The Quran, however, metes out justice and equity selectively. For example, in a court of law, a woman's word, is equal to half that of her male counterpart (Sura 4:34). This loophole can be very attractive to men who are accustomed to slapping women around and beating their wives, a practice that Sura 4:34 also defends. We need something better, something that will save us from such abuses. The New Testament has such a way, a way that maintains our oneness in Christ, no matter who we are. Consider the following illustration.

On one occasion, devout religious zealots caught a woman in the act of adultery and brought her to Jesus. Jesus turned to her male accusers who were ready to stone the shamefaced adulteress and said, "Whoever is without sin, let him cast the first stone." When they had all left, He spoke peace to her soul, "Woman, where are those accusers? . . . Neither do I condemn you; go and sin no more" (John 8 NKJV). This example of public salvation involved saving her life and her soul.

Public salvation also means being more concerned about eternal things such as forgiveness and mercy than about temporary things such as getting even and helping only yourself. Does that mean that the God of the Bible is not concerned about our daily bread? Of course not. But when we have eaten our bread, we soon discover that we are still unsatisfied. Too often we resort to eating someone else's bread as did the adulterous woman.

Jesus knew, however, that what she yearned for, what we all yearn for our entire lives, is something more, something of eternal value. Mistakenly, we sometimes latch onto faulty belief systems to fulfill our deepest yearnings. We believe that changing our name, donning Bedouin garb, chanting the Shahadah seven times a day, selling Power Products, and living a disciplined life (or even an adulterous life) will bring that sense of acceptance before the God of the Bible. But it won't.

The only thing that will open the door we have been knocking on our entire life is a personal and public relationship with Christ (Revelation 3:20). Only then will we be let into the party. There will be no need to seek a moment of glory from an adulterous relationship when we can get an eternity of glory from a relationship with the God of the Bible. We will begin to see our neighbors, Black and White, as people of value to be respected and honored, not as mortals, but as immortals (Lewis, 18).

At that point we will take each other more seriously. Yes, we will grieve and demand restitution for those who have abused us, White or Black, male or female. But we will also forgive, wanting only their restoration (as Jesus did this guilty woman) not wishing for any to remain in either a hellish existence or a hellish eternity.

How can we accomplish this you ask? How can we feel respect for someone who has disrespected us? How can we feel mercy for someone who has been unmerciful? We need a motivation that will tear down the walls that divide us. That motivation will be discussed in chapter 4.

4

A Motivation That Is Powerful

What's love got to do with it?
Tina Turner

What motivates us? What are the triggering factors behind our behaviors? Just why do we do the things we do? Fear is behind our every move: fear of abandonment; fear of exposure that we are, as everyone says, not worth loving; fear that we are incapable of dignity and unworthy of respect. Therefore, we disguise our actions to prevent our being found out (Crabb, 31-36).

Such was the case with Queen, great-grandmother of late author Alex Haley. From birth, this half-breed fought to avoid the stigma attached to being of interracial parentage. Wherever she turned, however, she was rejected because of her Irish complexion and other European features. At a very early age, she was taunted by the darker slave children for being a "high yellow."

Years later, she was relegated to the status of "house nigger" on the Forks plantation owned by her natural father, James Jackson, in Cypress, Alabama.

Following the Civil War, she insinuated herself upon the White residents of Decatur, Georgia, *who knew nothing about her biracial roots.* This masquerade led to a marital engagement with Lt. Digby, a White southern gentlemen, who, upon discovering Queen's true colors, violently beat and brutally raped her.

Left bleeding and wounded, Queen momentarily found love and acceptance with Davis, a handsome Black sharecropper in rural Georgia. After putting Queen in the family way, he abandoned his pregnant lover because of his own sense of unworthiness.

An unwed mother, Queen was then rejected by her religious employers, hell-bent on saving her fornicating soul. Feeling it was their Christian duty to protect Little Abner, her son, from his wanton mother, they determined to adopt her illegitimate son and leave this sinful maid behind.

Queen fled from these overzealous White spinsters' pan into the fires of the Ku-Klux Klan. These hooded night riders kidnapped Little Abner and torched his father's body as an object lesson to uppity Negroes. "Why do they hate us so much, Lord?" Queen sobbed, as the charred remains of her only love seared the young woman's soul. This strong-willed lady, who had once felt she could "kiss the tears away of every hurt Negro," was now left empty, bitter, and broken (Haley, 501).

Queen's dilemma of being hurt, rejected, and abused is not unlike the plight of countless Black Americans. From birth they have felt like they did not belong, that they had no place to go. They have been accustomed to sorrow and acquainted with grief by the abuses of society and their peers. The only way to deal with the pain is to turn either on yourself or on others.

Many, such as the Black Muslims, choose the latter. This other-directed contempt, however, goes deeper than the surface abuses it reflects. There is the ambivalence, disgust, and powerlessness felt toward society and the God who let it happen. This powerlessness breeds violence toward the violators, toward the people who turned a blind eye and said that your worth, dignity, and personhood are no big deal, toward people who refused to invest in ways to help Black Americans overcome self-destruction, toward people who maintain, "That happened to you over a century ago. Get over it!"

Dan Allender calls these people *abuser surrogates.* Like the mother who leads the eleven-year-old daughter into her father's bedroom, Christians and non-Christians who remain silent to the abuses of Black Americans socially, economically, and physically are partners in crime. Because of this silence, Black Americans have become vulnerable to anyone, including the Nation of Islam, who promises to assuage their pain and give them control over their lives.

But is embracing Minister Farrakhan's Power economic program the remedy to our growing powerlessness? Has not a similar "wonder drug" been tried and proven ineffective in places such as Russia, Korea, and China? Indeed, after walls had been torn down, after cities had been rebuilt, and after individuals had given their hearts and minds to an ideology of power, many still felt like invisible men and women. They still had feelings of purposelessness, wondering, "Who are we?" (Pannell, 104). Economic and social gains had been made externally, but the battle still raged internally.

Although the Nation of Islam has a good reputation for getting things done and turning things around on a short-term basis, recidivism (repeat crimes) among ex-offenders is still high. Black-on-Black crime still exists in mammoth proportions. Our cities are still filled with oppressed people, many of whom are waiting to explode at the slightest provocation.

External reforms will not work if internal changes have not been made. Ask Boris Yeltsin. These feelings of wrath harbored by oppressed individuals must be internally cut and rewired to avoid further self-destruction or destruction of others. Consider the following elaboration.

What's Eating You? Doctors who examine patients with colitis and ulcers not only try to discover what they have been eating but also what has been eating them. Troubling emotions eventually turn inward. Therefore, simply rejecting and resenting White devils is not the answer to your internal pain. Tagament ulcer medication will not make these unresolved issues subside.

Figure 1 diagrams the interaction of fear, bitterness, hate, anger, and resentment with one's body and soul. Such dominating problems will ultimately affect every avenue of your life.

For example, if your employer is White, your hatred for this so-called devil could affect your job performance. It could cloud your subordination to legitimate instructions. It could even lead you to explode and call him a racist even if there is no evidence to support your claim.

At home, this troubling emotion could motivate you to put Sura 4:34 into effect and beat your wife for having an opinion other than your own. At church, this hatred might cause you to reject the faith of your fathers, to label Christianity as the White man's religion, and thus to adopt the Muslim way of life. First John says that any man who hates his brother abides in death (John 4:20).

It does not list specifics. It does not give reasons. The God of the Bible knows that, no matter what precipitates it, bitterness will eat you up. Table 1 outlines some medical problems, such as migraines and colitis, which often accompany unresolved anger and bitterness.

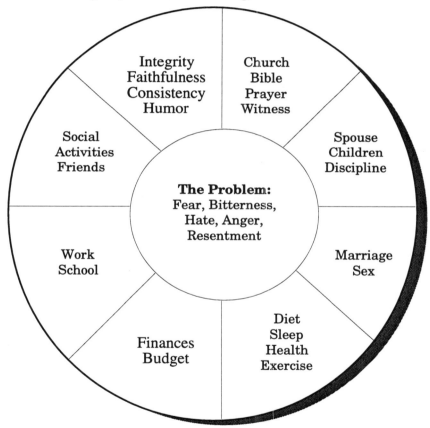

Figure 1. The Life-Dominating Problem.

This defensive style of relating (briefly discussed in chapters 1 and 2) does not protect you but rather makes you even more vulnerable.

> **Table 1. Physical Results of Anger**
>
> Hypothalamus gland secretes
> Pupils dilate
> Pituitary gland secretes
> Blood sugar level rises
> Adrenalin flows
> Breathing rate increases
> Heart rate increases
> Blood pressure increases
> Muscles tighten
> Digestion and elimination affected
> Breathing rate increases
> More air/oxygen enters lungs
> Blood clots faster

Ego Defenses. Like Queen, many children and adults resort to the following defenses to escape the anguish of being mistreated by someone in authority or someone you love:

- denial (my true religion is seventh-century Arabic)
- fantasy (Mr. Yacub's work)
- dissociation (with White and Black Americans)
- displacement (creating White devils)

These departures from reality (which, psychiatrists say, sometimes allow individuals to survive intolerable situations during childhood) are destroying the lives of many adults (Bradshaw, 74). To lead a healthy life, however, faulty beliefs must be replaced with hard truths.

The myth about the White devils is a case in point. Could this belief about Black America's arch enemy be the result in part of a story born from a displaced people tired of seeing their loved ones oppressed, rejected, and abused by those in power? Refuge is found in ego defenses that suggest the destruction of surrogates such as these. The fantasy goes something like this:

> *6,600 years ago, our nation gave birth, to another God whose name is Yacub. He changed civilization by creating a new race of people, who would climb like monkeys and rule the original Black nation for 6,000 years. These devils were really pale white with really blue eyes, which we think are the ugliest of colors. They were called Caucasian, which, according to Arab scholars, means ones whose evil effect is not confined to himself but affects others.* (Muhammad, 111)

This yarn is spun throughout the pages of *Message to the Black Man in America*, saying that Jesus gave up his work of trying to convert Jews and White devils to the religion of Islam. Mohammed was reportedly told that he could not reform these devils. They were driven out of Paradise into Europe.

The plot thickens when the Genesis account of creation is displaced with a new story about 59,999 White devils. A savior, Christ the Mahdi, is dispatched to destroy the wicked world of Caucasians and set up a world of peace with the Black man. Until then, the original Black Americans are warned about trusting these abusers of men, money, and power (Muhammad, 122). Using sixty-three biblical redefinitions of the White devils' identity, 128 redefinitions of the Black man's origin, and forty-two redefinitions of impending judgment of

White America, Farrakhan and his ministers have employed a classical revisionist approach to biblical history (See the appendix).

Impressionable Black Muslim converts are encouraged to digest this piece of fiction, which maintains that "Caucasians' pale skin and blue eyes are the tell-tale sign that there cannot be any sincere love and friendship with them." It goes on to say that "this race will always deceive the Black race who has a heart of gold and mercy" (Muhammad, 122).

Survival. If the above narrative is true, how can Black Americans survive this wicked race of people until the Mahdi returns? By wresting control? By usurping power? If they can just learn to help themselves, Minister Farrakhan and his mentor, Muhammad, insist that the White devil will never shame and mistreat them (like Queen) again. But will this hate-energized power heal, or will it ultimately kill twenty-eight million Black Americans' souls? That answer can only be found by facing the truth.

In order to know ourselves, we must be honest with ourselves. *Honesty*, according to Allender, admits that we have been deceived and would prefer to establish a false world rather than face the bright, searing light of truth. *Dishonesty*, on the other hand, is an attempt to dethrone the God of the Bible. It is an attempt to become the God of the Bible and construct an alternative world that spins to our own reality, the reality that maintains that White people are devils, the reality that holds that the so-called original race of Black Americans will one day rule the world (Allender, 183). This reality says, Unless you play by my rules, I'll take my marbles and play elsewhere, in a new separate African nation, in the land bequeathed to us by our ancestors.

However, it takes more energy to deny the truth than it does to unload the weight of a false world full of White devils that we have been bearing on our shoulders. Yes, the truth hurts, but it will also relieve our wounded hearts.

The truth is we have been victims. We have been violated economically by unfair practices, such as the FHA loan policies that excluded decades of Black Americans from adequate housing. We have been violated socially by the very agencies the God of the Bible ordained to protect our civil liberties, such as the more than 500 incidents of force and harassment by Los Angeles police officers who escaped prosecution in 1992. We have been violated psychologically by professors who devalue our young men and women at institutions of higher learning (Pannell, 94-99). Our response to that victimization has caused us to hurt and hate the violators as we have been hurt and hated. But once we face the truth, we will be able to repent.

"Repent?" you ask. "Repent about what? We have been patient. We have put up with Klan violence. We have been the underdog, the slaves. We have been kicked to the curb by police brutality. We are the first to be laid off because of double-digit inflation. Our heroes have been incarcerated. What do *we* have to repent about?"

Only one thing. Repent that we have clenched our fist at the God of the Bible for allowing the abuses of society to happen against our people. Repent that we have, like the Prodigal Son, decided to make life work on our own. Repent that we have developed a self-help policy and do not need a "White" God's help. Repent that we have created a god – be it a seventh-century pagan moon deity or the Black man himself – who will keep the White dogs at bay, a god who will keep the White devils from devaluing our young men whom they stick in the state penitentiary out of proportion to their participation in the criminal activity that abounds in these United States.

In this context, then, our anger is not at the White man. That is our performance problem. That is how we have acted out our rage and misdirected our resentment against a higher power. Our anger is at the God of the Bible. We replaced Him. He is now Allah, Farrakhan, Muhammad, Fard, and 360 other pagan deities at the Kabah. Like Mary, a close friend of Jesus, we have cried, "Lord, if you had been here, my brother would not have died. Malik would not have gone to prison. Malice would not have been beaten to death. Rodney would not have been denied his civil rights."

As Allender points out, the God of the Bible is seen as a games player, a cosmic sadist who twists the screws of pleasure to increase the pain of His victims. He is someone either to placate or to ignore (Allender, 212). Thus, we embrace a lifestyle of discipline such as al-Islam, where our passion is held in check. Our desires for intimacy and impact are regarded with indifference.

But humble repentance says that choosing false gods and denying the resurrection of Christ is a mockery of the cross. The God of the Bible proved His love for Black Americans 2,000 years ago on Mount Calvary. It was not the God of the Bible who hurt us. It was not skin that hurt us. It was, and still is, sin. And yet the love of the God of the Bible overcame this monster that destroys relationships, distorts the gospel, and deludes humankind. Can it overcome your hellish situation? Of course it can. The fact that it is the love of the God of the Bible and not a fabrication of White or Black devils makes it a positive change agent. Love motivates us to heal. Here's how.

What is Love? Love is a movement of supernatural grace that empowers us to move toward those who have offended us. It cancels the debt owed just as Jesus canceled our debts when He died a sacrificial death. This kind of unselfish love is exhibited in Luke 7, where Jesus tells of two men with financial trouble. The one debtor is hopelessly bankrupt, while the other has but a few credit card bills. What they have in common, however, is that both parties lack sufficient funds to settle their accounts. Therefore, the big-hearted creditor forgives both debts when he realizes their bind.

After telling the parable, Jesus turns to His host, a religious conservative, and asks, "Simon, which person do you think loves the creditor most?" Simon replies, "The one to whom the creditor forgave the most debt." Jesus applauds Simon's accurate assessment. He then tells him about an immoral woman and a religious person. The woman has lived an immoral life. The religious person has kept the law, fasted, prayed, and given alms.

This he tells in reference to a distraught woman who has knelt at Jesus' feet, the dirtiest part of His body, washed them with her tears, and wiped them with the hair of her head. The religious Simon had been smugly thinking that if this "Savior" had the wherewithal to know what kind of a foul, frivolous woman she was, He would not allow her to touch his person. Jesus made his point, however, that the woman, representing so many of us whose sins are many, loves more. At the same time, Simon, representing so many religious persons wrapped up in their own self-righteousness, deluding themselves that they have very little sin, actually have very little love.

Let's apply this parable to twenty-eight million Black Americans. Using Muhammad's logic in his *Message to the Black Man,* we will assume that Blacks are inherently good and Whites are inherently bad. Therefore, we can deduce that White devils have a far bigger bill than the God of the Bible's "original race." They have raped, kidnapped, and lynched. They have enslaved. They have discriminated. Their tab is tremendous. But is that a fair assessment? Does all this add up? Does not the Lord's prayer say, "Forgive us our debts as we forgive our debtors"? Following biblical logic, then, does not our unwillingness to forgive White Americans' atrocities put us in arrears in the books of heaven? Has not our refusal to love this so-called fallen race given us a bad credit rating?

Jesus taught us to love our enemies and to pray for those who despitefully use us (Matthew 5:44). No one has suffered more than He. Therefore, Jesus spoke from experience. He chose to leave heaven and show us how to have an intimate relationship with the God of the Bible and a loving relationship with humankind. He was the offended pursuing the offender. We could not earn His gift of love. We did not deserve His gift of love. He just gave it to us freely. He wants us to do the same.

Power of Love. Jesus knew that the greatest power on earth and in heaven is the power of love. Yes, at times love must be tough. At other times it must be tender. Love is not a doormat. It is a choice. Jesus chose to lay His life down for us. And every day we choose or do not choose to do the same for our fellows, Black or White.

This choice to love means you resist the temptation to hate. You do not take vengeance in your own hands. You give up your right to retaliate. This does not imply that you have no rights, that you do not take a stand against evil. Jesus himself resisted the profaning of God's temple by moneychangers, physically driving them out (Matthew 21:12). Paul opposed Peter when he compromised biblical truths (Galatians 2:11). In fact, God gave us civil government to avenge evil practices, including brutal beatings on the highways and the rape of our children (Romans 13). It is our duty to report crime. To excuse it or to belittle wrongdoing, such as 500 acts of police brutality, is not an act of love, but an act of wickedness.

The full gospel includes not only God's love and mercy but His righteousness, justice, and eternal punishment as well. Laws are given to protect us from the terrors of evil, including law enforcement agents who suspect every Black man of being guilty. The loving thing is to hold them accountable, to request a second trial. If the law does not work for the least of us, it will not work for the best of us. When these God-ordained protection agencies are ignored and become instruments of unrighteousness, people become vigilantes. They take the law into their own hands. It is in this soil that a Farrakhan can grow the weeds of dissent and revenge. Who can blame them? No one else would protect their interests. Perhaps this self-styled "god-man" will.

Nonetheless, the Bible, the older document, from which this angel of light quotes extensively, says that when we are hit on one cheek we are to turn the other cheek to our enemies, a definite non-avenging, non-retaliatory, humble action. " 'Vengeance is Mine [not Farrakhan's], I will repay,' says the Lord" (Romans 12:19). The God of the Bible will commit to protecting us if we will commit to loving others. Whether with our neighbor, our boss, our wife, or our enemy, the power of love can restore, rebuild, and reconcile.

Love is the real fulfillment of the law many mistaken Black Muslims are trying to keep. If you love, you will not cheat your neighbor. You will not take his wife. You will not mistreat your boss. You will forgive your debtors. Loving, then, is risky business. How about it Black Muslim? If the God of the Bible ran a credit check on you today, what would it say? Would it show certain parts of the God of the Bible's body, such as White Americans, whom you refuse to love because they are putrid and despicable in their dealings with Black Americans? Are there any overdue bills marked "Unresolved bitterness toward your White employer"? How many times have you thrown your insubordinate wife on the bed, like the Quran says, and beat her into submission? Are you delinquent in repaying your bill of mercilessness?

Instead of falling down at Jesus' feet and weeping, some proudly recite the Shahadah. Indeed, it is easier to deny the resurrection and hate the White devil than face the truth about our refusal to love our brother, White or Black, as ourselves. Muhammad admonishes Black Muslims to love themselves (Muhammad, 32). However, Jesus knew that most of us love ourselves too much already. It is humankind whom we have problems loving – especially those whom we deem our enemies.

According to the Quran you are not to love your enemy if you wish to be a true Muslim. But Jesus says to love your enemy (Matthew 5:46). He goes on to say that if you love only those who love you, what's the big deal? Even heathen people love people who love them. Real power is a product of loving those who have abused, hurt, and rejected you. This motivation comes from within and is born of a commitment to love and not to fear. Even though Jesus' followers have not always demonstrated love, Jesus did, setting the example for us to follow.

Greater love has no man than this, that a man lay down his life for his friends. Jesus died for the just and for the unjust. He knew what was in the hearts of men, that our hearts are stony, in open defiance of the God of the Bible and our neighbor. Yet He came to replace it with a heart of forgiveness, a tender heart of flesh.

What's love got to do with it, Black Muslim? Love is our salvation. Love beats hate. Love beats retaliation. If, as Pannell noted, "our cities are full of walking, talking, driving, and sitting-next-to-you-at-the-ball-game time bombs," can we afford to embrace a religion that has a history of violence? Is not this like putting a .357 magnum in the hands of a child? Untrained in firearm safety, he or she is liable to shoot someone's head off. Has there not been enough blood shed, enough gang violence already? Should we now enlist to fight our own *Jihad,* our own holy war?

Indeed, early Islamic nations made their wealth by plundering weaker nations (Dashti, 184). Minister Farrakhan and His predecessors want to be just like them. They want to be equal with their oppressors, but equal in what, we might ask? Equal in buying 66,666,000 handguns? Or 72,739,000 rifles? That's what the average American citizen is packing these days according to the Bureau of Alcohol, Tobacco, and Firearms (Pannell, 96).

Or maybe, as Dr. Alvin Poussaint suggests, we want to follow the Rambo mentality that sanctions aggressivity – that teaches our children that violence solves problems, that if you do not agree with me, I will kill you (as many Muslims still do for their faith).

What's wrong with a little ethnic cleansing every now and again, committing unspeakable acts of violence against innocent women in the name of religion? Is this what we want for ourselves? Or perhaps we prefer the white collar crimes of, say, convicted financier Michael Milken. Would we prefer to wield our power on Wall Street, however short-lived?

Milken and so many others got their land, money, status, and power the old-fashioned way – by dishonesty. Yet they are still unhappy. They may say *as-salaam aleikum,* but there is no peace, no love within. Consider the rash of hatred and violence that erupted between 1970 and 1993 involving Black Muslims:

- •1970 Bookstore in Philadelphia firebombed for having a Malcolm X poster in its window.
- •1971 One-hundred-person brawl erupted between Muslims and Black Panthers over turf rights for selling newspapers.
- •1972 New York's Temple #7 has three-hour shoot out.
- •1972 Factions in New York implicated in assassinations of out-spoken followers of Malcolm.
- •1973 Seven Hanafis (rival sect) murdered over theological dispute. Five of the victims were children, including babies who were drowned in the bathtub.
- •1984 Farrakhan threatens to make an example of *Washington Post* reporter, Milton Coleman, who disclosed Jesse Jackson's "Hymietown" remark. (He later denies calling for the reporter's death.)
- •1984 Farrakhan calls for race war to erupt in 1986.
- •1991 Farrakhan asks audience at Savior's Day parade if they are willing to kill for Islam.
- •1992 Nation of Yahweh (Black Muslim group) tried for killing fourteen persons in Miami in the 1980s.
- •1993 Black Muslim Daniel Green arraigned for murder of Michael Jordan's father, James (*Dateline*). Daniel and his white accomplice posed for a video flashing the silver NBA championship ring the elder Jordan had been wearing, a gift from his superstar son.

If we continue on this path, will we be any better than the Sadaam Husseins who kill in the name of religion? Will we be better than the Muammar Qadaffis or the Manuel Noriegas? Violence does not breed character or power. It breeds more violence. Unlike Minister Farrakhan, Jesus knew the power of love. It motivated

Him to die for His enemies. It put an end to the feud. Because of Christ's sacrificial death and resurrection, an eye for an eye was replaced with love for those who disagree with you.

Imagine Jesus calling for, as the Quran does, the killing of all who follow different teachings (Morey, 38). Imagine Jesus insinuating, as Minister Farrakhan did of Malcolm X, that all who follow another sect are worthy of death. No, Jesus chose a better way to deal with opposition. He chose not to retaliate. He chose to love. He left vengeance up to the God of the Bible who alone can exact perfect justice, perfect retribution. He knew the devastation that inner and outer hate could bring, as psychiatrist John Powell so aptly describes:

> *The evidence for the crippling effects of a loveless life is found in the office of every psychiatrist, filled with children and adults who have no awareness of their own worth, no sense of identity, people who are filled with hatred and fear and tortured by anxieties. Love is costly, but the alternatives are deadly.* (Powell, 97)

Our people need salvation. They do not need violence. They need a positive alternative to their hellish volatile situation. They have run out of choices. Only two remain: Islam and the Judeo-Christian ethic. Choose this day, Black person, whom you will serve: the gods of a murderous, pagan, seventh-century moon cult or the redefined gods that Minister Farrakhan serves or the God of the Bible. As for me and my house, we will serve the God of the Bible. We will serve the God of *hesed*, unconditional steadfast love. We will serve the resurrected Christ. We will serve the Lord.

FARRAKHAN INTERPRETS THE HOLY BIBLE

When interpreting and applying Scripture, there are several rules that must be followed:

1. The Bible is authoritative. Tradition and earthly reason are to take a back seat.
2. The Bible (not the Quran or the *Hadith*) best interprets itself.
3. Saving faith and the inspiration of God's Holy Spirit are necessary to understand and properly interpret the Scriptures (Henrichsen, 147-155).

To this latter point, the Bible, the older document, maintains that without God's Spirit indwelling any interpreter (as a result of a personal saving relationship with Jesus Christ) the natural man (such as Minister Farrakhan) is unable to see – much less accept – the things that come from the God of the Bible. Such matters as the virgin birth of Jesus are foolishness to him. He cannot understand them because they are spiritually discerned. Unfortunately, Farrakhan does not believe in spirits, or spooks as he calls them. He is, therefore, unable to properly interpret the Bible (1 Corinthians 2:14).

Cultists are experts at lifting texts out of their respective contexts without proper regard for either the laws of language or the established principles of biblical interpretation. They are among those of whom 2 Peter 3:16 warns, who "wrest . . . the Scriptures unto their own destruction" (Martin, 23).

Following is a sampler of some cultic liberties that Minister Farrakhan takes with his applications of biblical truth. There is no recognized school of theology that supports these applications.

Theme: Allah (God) Is a Man!

Farrakhan's Version	Scriptural Truth
Allah (God) is a man in reality, and not a spirit.	Many deceivers confess not that Jesus Christ is come into the world. This is a deceiver and an antichrist (Rev. 1:7).
Allah (God) is a flesh and blood human being.	And the Word became flesh, and dwelt among us (Gen. 6:3; John 1:14).

Theme: Isa (Jesus) Historically and Prophetically

Farrakhan's Version	Scriptural Truth
Jesus was of the seed of David according to the flesh.	Concerning His Son, who was born of a descendant of David according to the flesh, who was declared the Son of God with power by the resurrection from the dead, according to the spirit of holiness . . . (Rom. 1:3).

Theme: True Identity of Satan, the Devil, Revealed
Farrakhan's Version   Scriptural Truth

Farrakhan's Version	Scriptural Truth
Integration with the devil (White race) will not last.	Woe to the earth and the sea, because the devil has come down to you, having great wrath, knowing he has only a short time (Isa. 29:17-18).

Theme: Signs of Judgment According to the Bible
Farrakhan's Version   Scriptural Truth

Farrakhan's Version	Scriptural Truth
There is no life after physical death.	When a cloud vanishes, it is gone, So he who goes down to Sheol does not come up (Job 7:9-10).

Theme: Mystery of Babylon Revealed as America
Farrakhan's Version   Scriptural Truth

Farrakhan's Version	Scriptural Truth
America is where the eagle (Satan) and the carcass (mentally dead Black people) are gathered together.	Where the corpse is, there the vultures will gather (Matt. 24:28).

FOR FURTHER STUDY

Al Haadi Al Mahdi, Isa. *What and Where Is Hell?* Brooklyn: Ansaary Allah, 1986.

Allender, Dan B., and Larry Crabb. *Encouragement: The key to Caring.* Grand Rapids: NavPress, 1990.

_____. *Wounded Heart.* Colorado Springs: NavPress, 1990.

Bradshaw, John. *Healing the Shame That Binds You.* Deerfield Beach, Fl.: Health Communications, 1988.

Dashti, Ali. *Twenty-three Years: A Study of the Prophetic Career of Mohammad.* London, England: George Allen & Unwin, 1985.

Dateline, NBC. August 24, 1993.

Guthrie, Stan. "A Crescent for a Cross," *Christianity Today,* October 2, 1991, p. 40.

Haley, Alex, and David Stevens. *Queen.* New York: William Morrow, 1993.

Hall, Mimi. "Key Questions Linger: Why?" *USA Today,* April 20, 1993, p. 2A.

Hanagraph, Hank. Unpublished interview with Robert Morey. San Juan Capistrano: KKLA Radio, 1992.

Henrichsen, Walter, and Gayle Jackson. *Studying, Interpreting, and Applying the Bible.* Grand Rapids: Zondervan, 1990.

Karrupa, Dave. "Hate Story: Farrakhan's Still at it," *New Republic,* May 30, 1988, pp. 19-22.

Kramer, Michael. "The Charmer," *New York,* October 7, 1985, p. 16(3).

Lewis, Bernard. *Race and Color in Islam.* New York: Octagon, 1979.

Lewis, C. S. *The Weight of Glory.* New York: Collier Books, Macmillan, 1962.

Mandelbaum, Allen. *Divine Comedy of Dante Alighieri: Inferno.* New York: Bantam, 1980.

Martin, Walter. *The Kingdom of the Cults.* Minneapolis: Bethany House, 1965.

McClintock, John, and James Strong. *Cyclopedia of Biblical, Theological, and Ecclesiastical Literature.* Grand Rapids: Baker, 1981.

McDowell, Josh. *Evidence That Demands a Verdict.* San Bernadino: Here's Life, 1972.

Mills, Barbara. "Louis Farrakhan Envisions African Homeland for U.S. Blacks," *People Weekly,* September 17, 1990, pp. 111-115.

Morey, Robert. *The Islamic Invasion.* Eugene, Oregon: Harvest House, 1992.

Muhammad, Elijah. *Message to the Black Man in America.* Philadelphia: Hakims Publication, 1965.

Pannell, William. *The Coming Race Wars.* Grand Rapids: Zondervan, 1993.

Parry, Alan, and Linda Parry. *The Evergreen Wood.* Nashville: Nelson, 1992

Powell, John. *Unconditional Love.* Allen, Texas: Tabor, 1978.

Puente, Maria. "Koresh Ruled with Scripture, Fear, and Charisma," *USA Today,* April 20, 1993, p. 2.

Reed, Adolph. "The Rise of Louis Farrakhan," *Nation*, January 21, 1991, pp. 37-54.

Roebuck, Paul. *Islamic Cult Packet*. Unpublished private communication, 1993.

Russell, Diane E. H. *The Secret Trauma*. New York: Basic Books, 1986.

Salley, Columbus, and Ronald Behm. *What Color Is Your God?* Downers Grove: InterVarsity, 1970.

Sanders, C. *Introduction to Research in English Literary History*. New York: Macmillan, 1952.

Turque, Bill, Vern E. Smith and John McCormick. "Playing a Different Tune: Louis Farrakhan is trying to reach out to the white mainstream," *Newsweek,* June 28, 1993, pp. 30-31.

Tyson Documentary. USA Network, March 1993.

Waldron, Clarence. "Blacks Take a Look at Cults." *Jet*. Chicago: Johnson, May 10, 1993.

Wood, Leon J. *The Prophets of Israel*. Grand Rapids: Baker, 1979.

Moody Press, a ministry of the Moody Bible Institute, is designed for education, evangelization, and edification. If we may assist you in knowing more about Christ and the Christian life, please write us without obligation:

Moody Press, c/o MLM,
Chicago, Illinois 60610.